God's Fantastic Creatures

By Sally Streib

Illustrated by Rebecca Gadway

Sea n' See Presentations
Teaching kids of all ages to know and love their God.
www.seansee.net
Copyright © 2019 Sally Streib and Sea n' See Presentations
ISBN: 978-0-9711104-7-2

SEAWAY
BOOKS

Cover and book design by David Valentin.

Bible verses quoted are used by permission from The Clear Word.
Copyright © 1994 by Jack J. Blanco
These stories are all true and the people are real.

AIM HIGHER
AVID INK MEDIA

Seaway Books are published by Avid Ink Media, a division of Big Idea Development Center, LLC Encinitas California

TABLE OF CONTENTS

We love God because He first loved us.
That's where our love comes from.

1 John 4:19

Prickly Sea Urchins and Triggerfish

Sea urchins are not my favorite creatures. They're covered with long spines that can get stuck in my skin. They also have many foolish habits.

God loves all His creatures and teaches them how to stay safe. That includes sea urchins.

All night urchins ooze over the sand looking for food. They know they must head back to their safe caves before the sun rises. Sometimes urchins will choose to stay out of their caves and sit on the sand in plain sight.

The triggerfish is the urchin's enemy. They grab a spine, carry the urchin to the surface of the sea and drop it. The urchin turns over and over as it falls, and lands on the sand on its back.

Triggerfish will swim over to the upside down urchin, purse their lips, and suck out the urchin's flesh through a small opening that is unprotected.

God loves us and has taught us how to stay safe from our enemy, Satan. We aren't covered with spines and we don't hide in caves. We can choose to be covered by God's love. We are safe with Him.

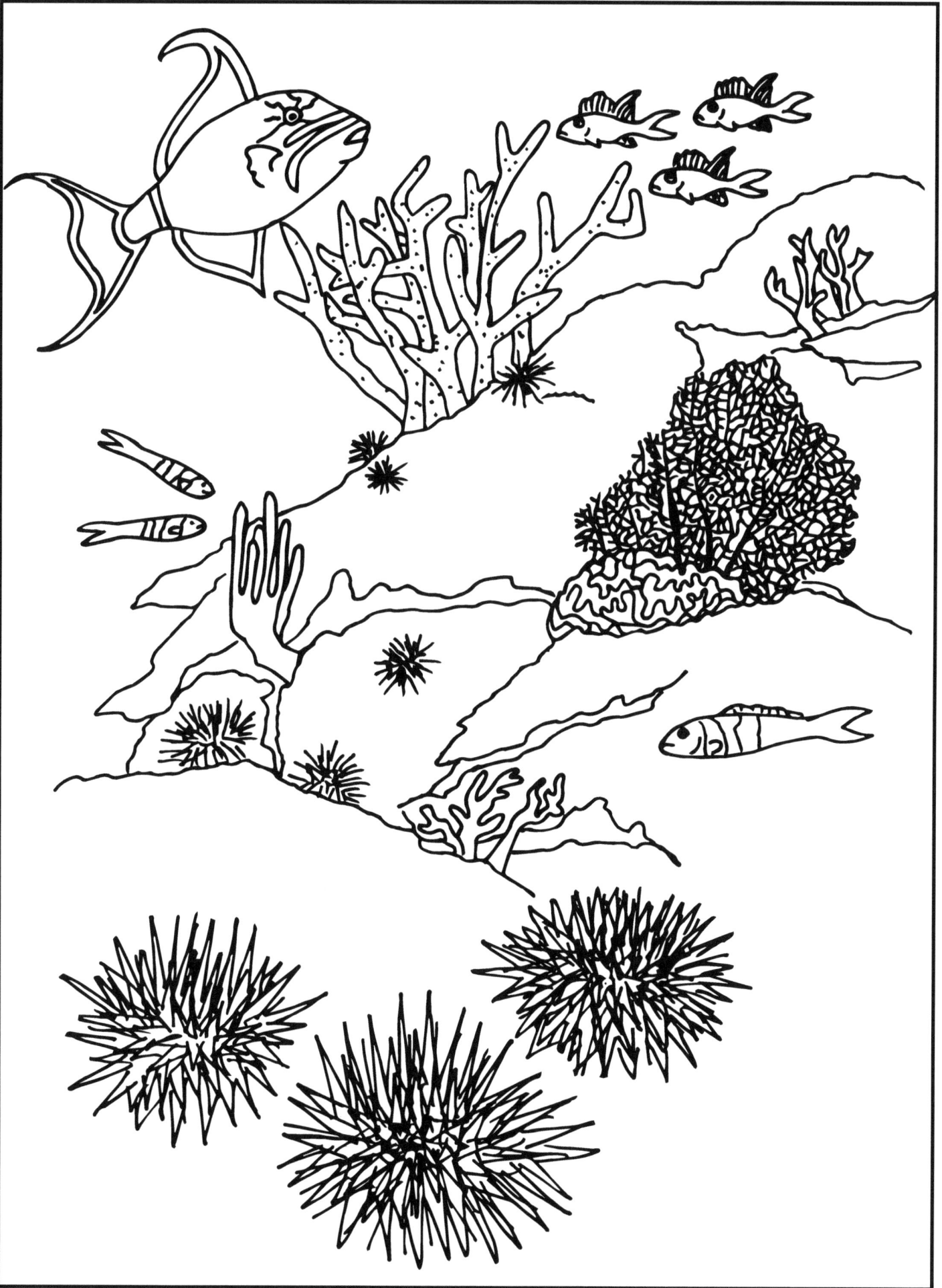

If we confess our sins, He is faithful and just to forgive us our sin and to clean us up from all unrighteousness.

1 John 1:9

Be Careful With Cone Shells

I spotted a brightly colored shell the shape of a miniature ice-cream cone while diving in the South Pacific Islands. I reached down to pick it up. "Don't touch that thing!" a voice inside my brain screamed. I yanked my hand back and stared. I remembered that the poison-tipped harpoon inside the cone could kill.

A small fish hovered over the cone shell. Maybe it thought the cone was just a piece of coral or a little rock. But suddenly, bam! A tiny dart shot out of the shell, it plunged into the fish and it hung there helpless. How will the cone eat that fish, I wondered.

Suddenly a tube stuck out of the cone shell. It stretched around the fish and swallowed it up. It took a lot of time and a lot of stretching, but eventually the fish disappeared into the tube. Gulp! It was gone.

Our enemy, Satan, shoots his temptations at us. Bam! We get stung. But, there's good news! Scientists don't have an antidote for many of the cone shell's stings. But our God sent Jesus to become one for us.

Don't touch Satan's stuff, but if you get stung and sin, let Jesus' forgiveness be your saving antidote. Remember what John tells us in John 1:9.

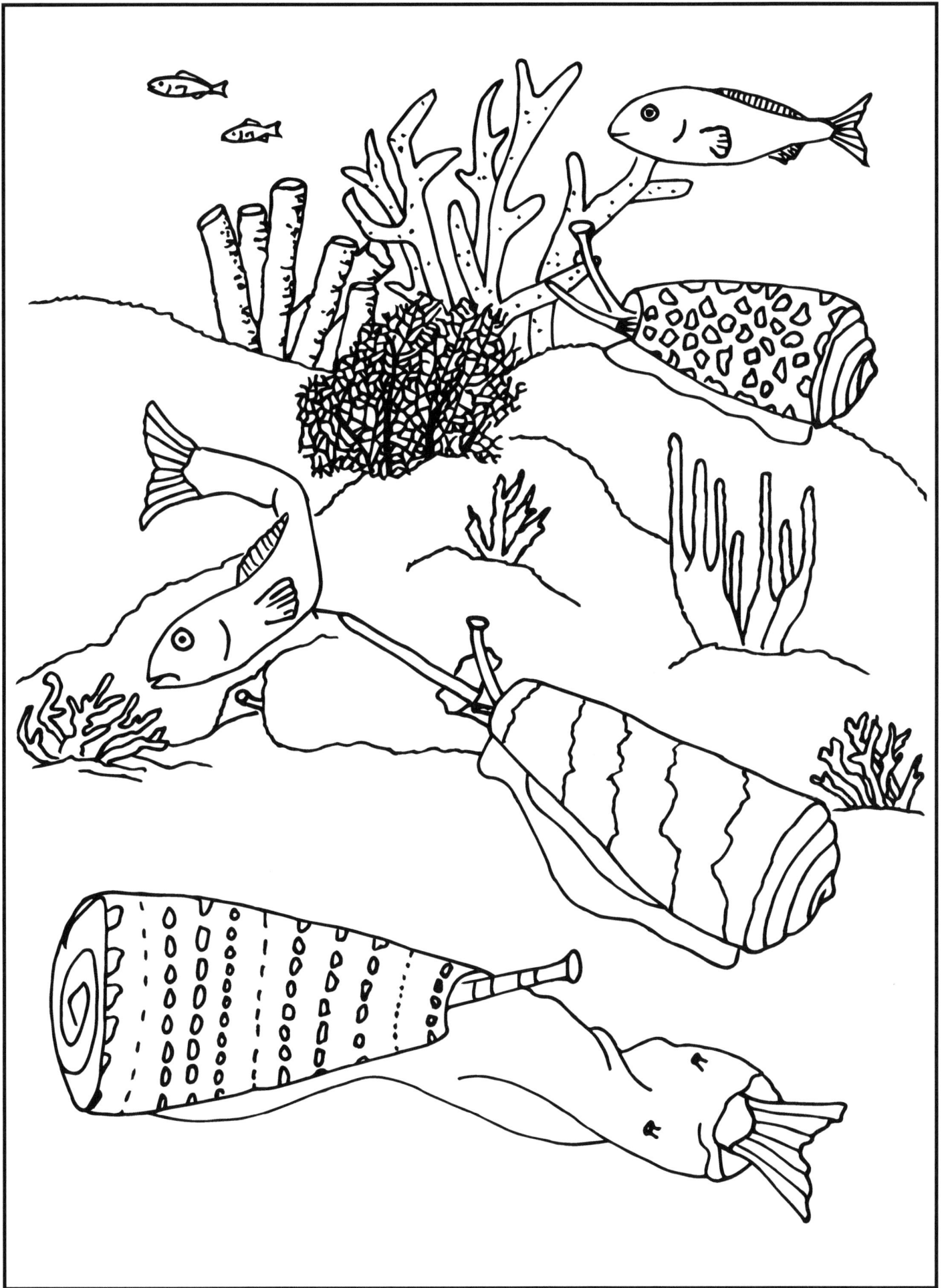

Grace and peace to you from Jesus Christ, God's faithful witness, the first One given sovereignty over death by His resurrection and who is the rightful Ruler over all kings in the world. He is the One who loves us and has freed us from our sins by His own blood.

Revelation 1:5

~OR~

The Huge Horse Conch

Martha, my dive buddy, walked ahead of me across the mud flats on Sanibel Island, Florida.

"I found a horse conch," she shouted holding up a huge shell. When she saw hardened mud, barnacles and algae all over it, she threw it down into the mud. "I want to find a good one," she said. I picked up the Horse Conch and tucked it into my pack.

Martha found a second horse conch. She threw it down, too, because it had the same ugly stuff all over it. When she walked on, I picked up that shell.

Later, in our cottage, I cleaned one shell and rubbed it down with a mixture of baby oil and lighter fluid. It looked beautiful.

When Martha got up, she saw the clean horse conch and asked me if she could have it back. "No," I said, "I rescued it and cleaned it and I'm going to take it home."

Satan thought that when God saw the barnacles and mud of sin on us, He would throw us away. But, He didn't. He rescues us, cleans us and will take us home someday.

~OR~

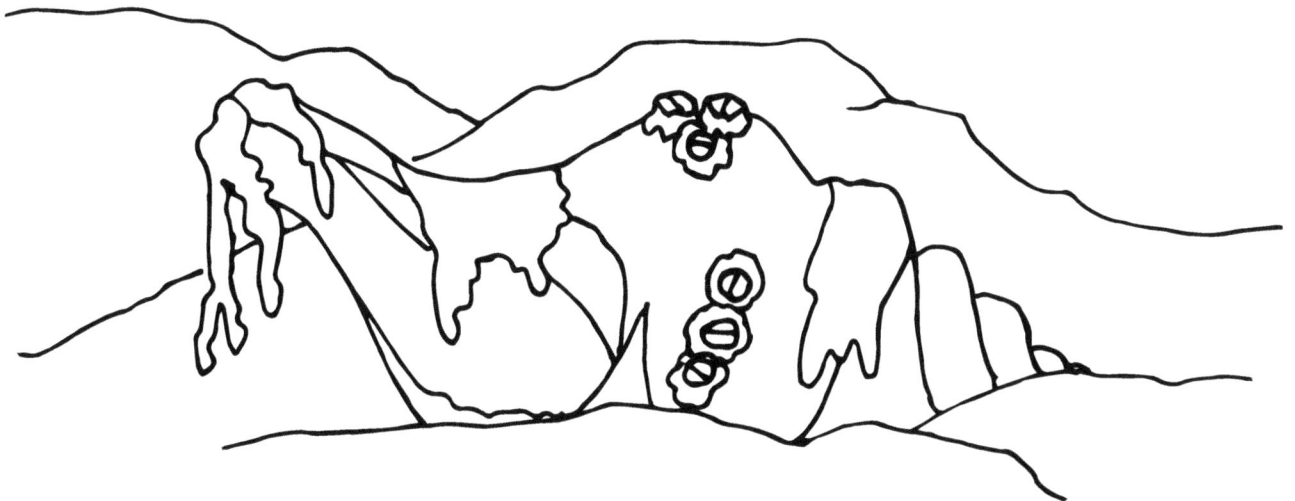

You need to submit your will to God. Resist the devil, and he'll flee from you. Stay close to God and He'll stay close to you.

James 4:7-8

Stars in the Sea

Piaster, the California sea star, lives on the rocky cliffs where waves crash and pound it all day. It has to cling to the rocks, so God gave it hundreds of little suction cups.

Piaster also has to stay free from clinging creatures, like barnacles. I've never seen one Piaster star with anything attached to it because God covered its back with tiny pinchers. It uses these to pinch any creature that comes too close.

Imagine how heavy a sea star could get with barnacles and shells and crabs hanging off it as it tries to stick to the rocky cliffs.

We are God's stars. He knows that Satan will try to get his temptations to attach to us as we cling to Him. We can't pinch him, but we can do something that works just as good.

When we feel tempted to do something we know isn't right, we can just say the name of Jesus. Satan hears that name and it is just like a good pinch! James 4:7 tells us that Satan will actually flee from us. I like that idea!

Trust in the Lord forever, for the Lord Jehova is an eternal rock, the Rock of all ages.

Isaiah 26:4

The Amazing Abalone

The abalone shell is an amazing creature. It clings to a rocky cliff with a suction cup that never gets tired. Even when big waves smash against it, the abalone does not fall off. It sticks tight.

When I found my first abalone, I said, "This is not a very pretty shell." The outside looked just like a rock. But the inside surprised me. I saw a swirl of red, blue, green, gold and purple colors.

Now I know to hold the abalone shell up toward the sun and watch all the colors shine. I learned that the closer I look, the more beauty I will see.

I know that Jesus made the abalone shell to show us that we can stick to Him with the power of love just like the abalone sticks to the rocks. And the more time we spend learning about Jesus and talking to Him, the more beautiful He looks. In His heart there is kindness and love and forgiveness that shine just like the beautiful colors inside the abalone shell.

Your word is a lamp for my feet and a light for my path.

Psalm 119:105

The Gorgeous Gaudy

Most seashells are creamy white, tan or pink to help them hide from enemies. Not the Gaudy Asephas shells.

I discovered them scattered along the shore in the Bahamas. I picked up empty purple, bright pink and white gaudy shells and dropped them into my yellow collecting bucket. These shells are gorgeous, I thought.

God wanted them to be noticed. He did not hide them. He placed them just beneath the sand along the shore. He wanted His sea creatures to have lots of food so they could become strong. He placed these shells right where they would be seen by their bright colors and enjoyed.

Our Bible is like that. God doesn't want it to be hidden. He wants His words to be noticed and read. If you look around, you will see Bibles everywhere.

The words in the Bible nourish and feed our hearts just like the Gaudy Asephas shells provide food for the sea creatures. Each word goes into our minds and gives us happy thoughts and courage. Each word helps us to become strong for God.

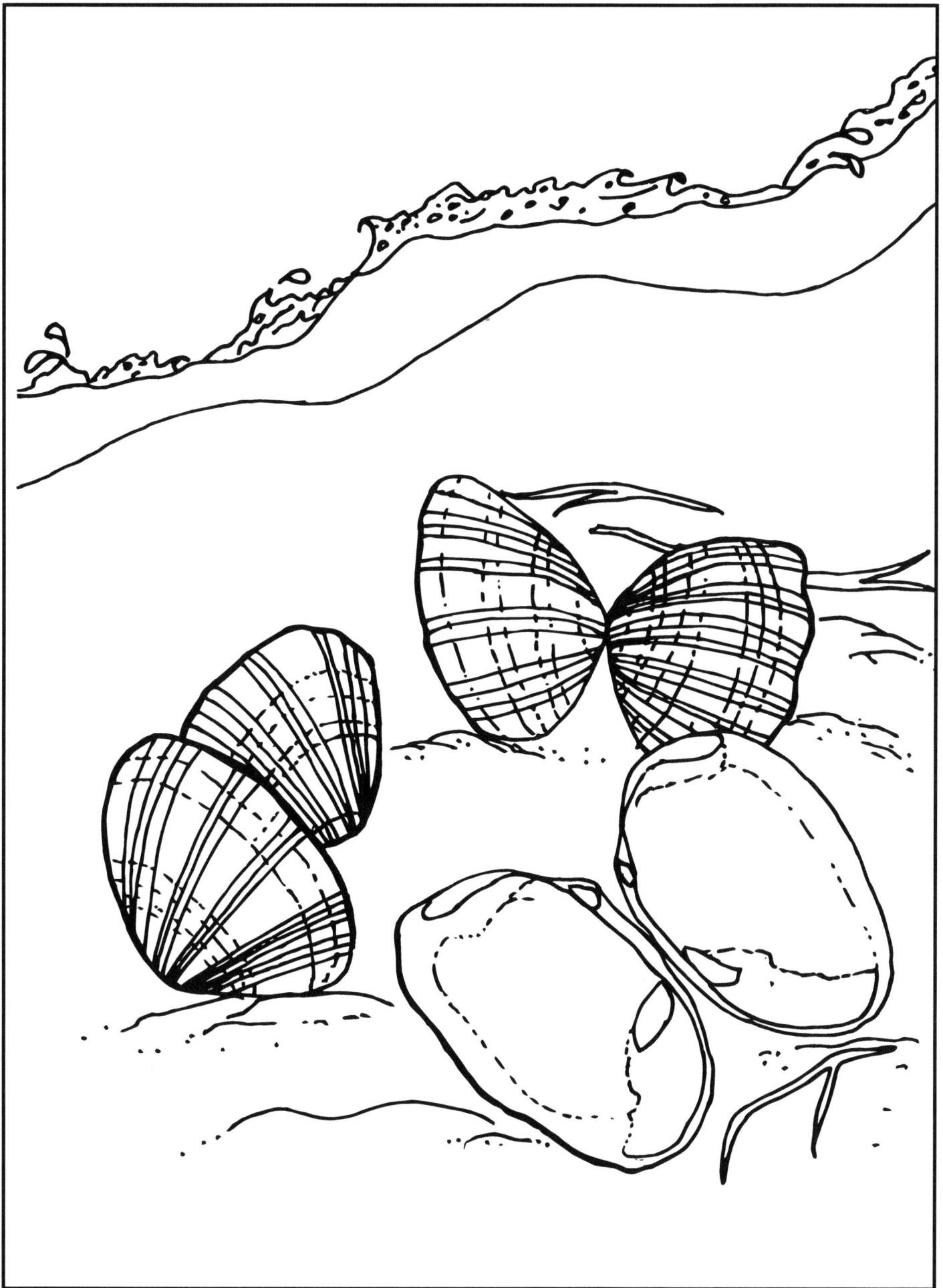

God's divine power has given us everything we need to live a Christian life, plus a knowledge of His goodness and glory.

2 Peter 1:3

Scallop Shell Power

I lay in the cold water just off Cape Cod with a snorkel jammed in my mouth. "There isn't a single shell around here," I mumbled, thrashing my hands around. Suddenly, all around me, hundreds of small shells burst up from the sand.

"Those are scallop shells!" I shouted into my snorkel.

I could see that the scallops had two sides that fit together. They opened the top of their shells and sucked in water. Click! A scallop close to me shut both shells together. I heard hundreds of clicks.

Suddenly each scallop opened at the bottom and shot water out a tiny tube. That lifted the shell up and away from me. When their shells became empty, they fell toward the sand. They filled with water again, shot it out and leaped away.

Those scallops have an ocean of power around them. So do we! We can take in God's power to help us trust and obey Him. Just as the scallops never run out of ocean water to help them leap, we won't run out of God's power.

I delight greatly in the Lord and my soul rejoices in my God. He has clothed me with the garments of salvation and covered me with the robe of righteousness. He has dressed me like a bridegroom and adorned me like a bride.

Isaiah 61:10

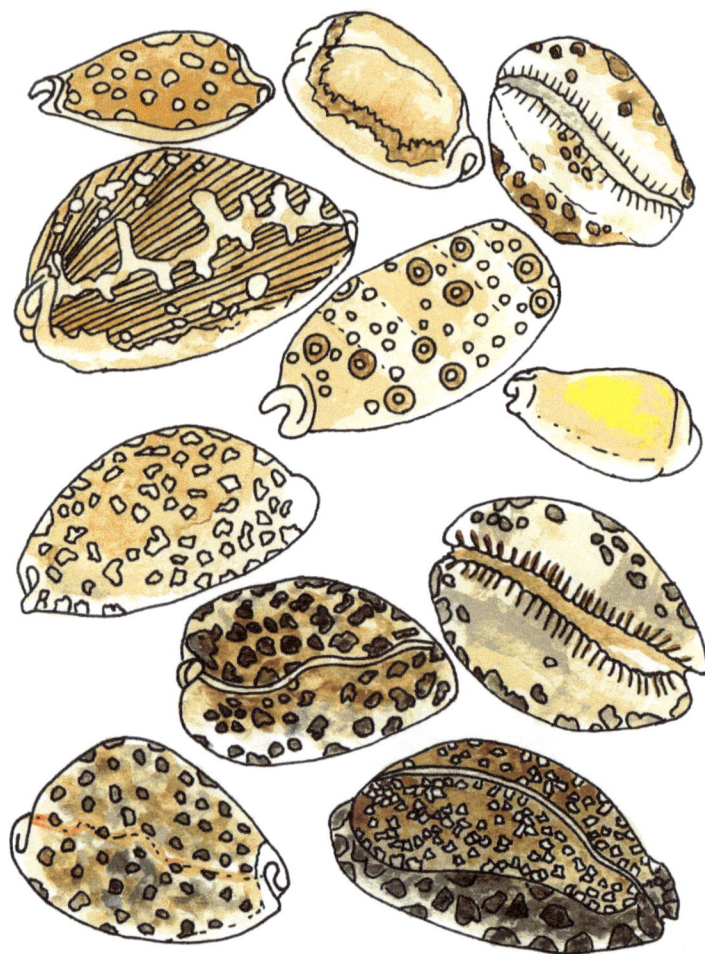

The Colorful Cowrie

While SCUBA diving in Hawaii, I spied a shiny cowrie shell oozing across the sand. That cowrie should be clinging to the underside of a rock, I thought.

Just then, a big, hairy crab came prancing by. It saw the cowrie shell and ran sideways toward it.

That cowrie is in big trouble, I thought. A crab can run faster than a cowrie can ooze.

The crab ran right up to the cowrie and tried to grab hold of it.

I expected to hear a loud crunching sound, but to my surprise, the crab's claw slipped right off the cowrie. The crab moved backwards and dashed for the cowrie shell again.

The cowrie simply wrapped itself in a thin covering called the mantle. It's slick and it's slimy. The claw just slid right off. The crab turned and ran back into its cave, pouting.

God has us covered, too. He gives us a covering called the "robe of righteousness, or goodness." When covered, Satan's temptations can't get a hold on us. They slip right off. That's why we shine like the beautiful cowrie.

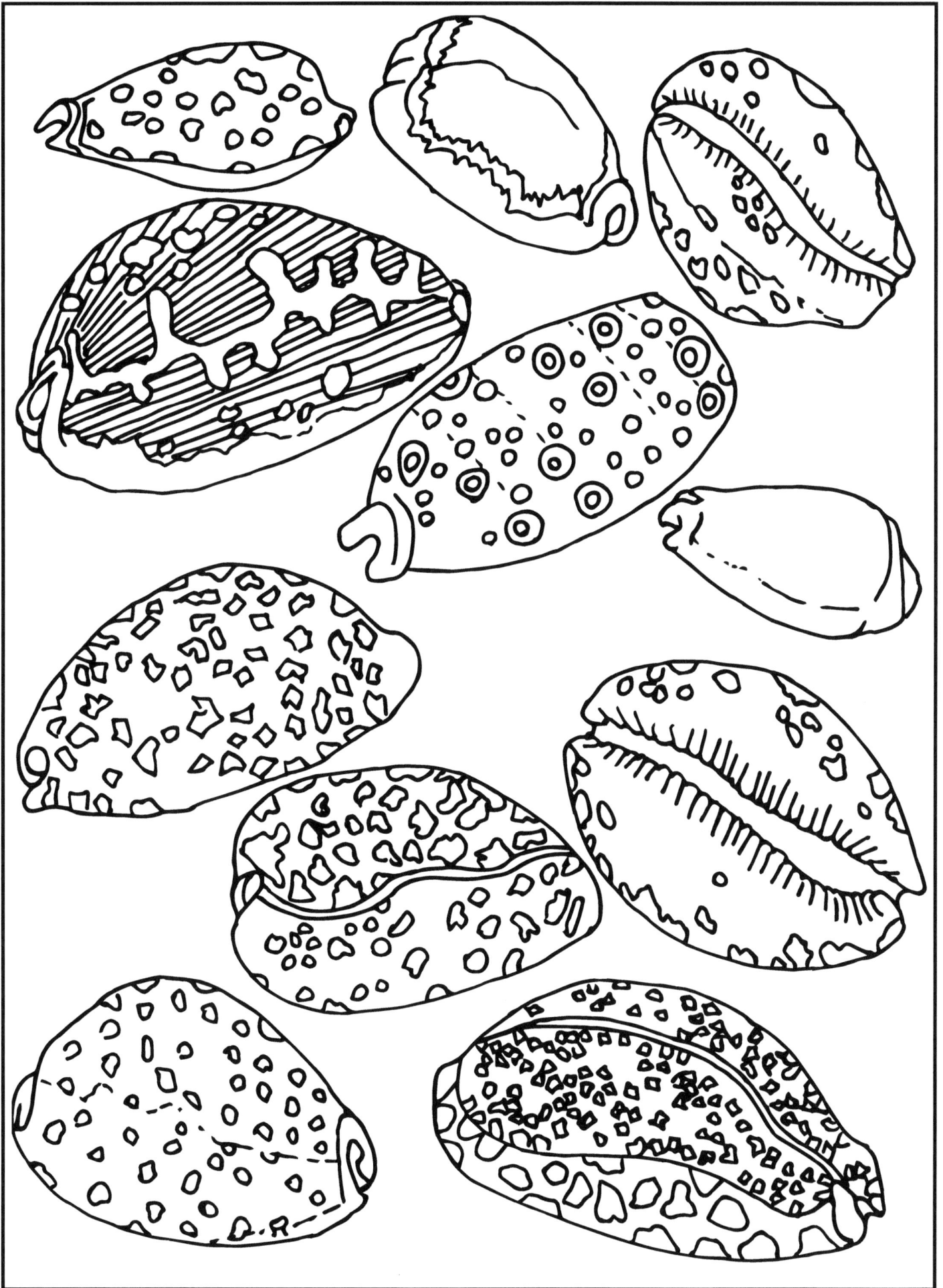

The angels of the Lord camp around those who reverence Him and deliver them.
Psalm 34:7

Rainbow Parrotfish in a Bubble

The Rainbow Parrotfish has scales that flash rainbow colors and teeth that make its mouth look like a parrot.

One day, while SCUBA diving, I swam right up to a beautiful Rainbow Parrotfish. My dive buddy motioned for me to move away so he could spear it. I shook my head, no. He finally swam away.

That night I read about parrotfish. I discovered a miracle. I learned that this beautiful fish has a scent that says to a passing predator fish, "Come on over and eat me. I taste good." That made me sad.

Then I learned that Rainbow Parrotfish are not afraid to go to sleep each night because of a miracle. God taught them to blow a bubble around themselves. Predator fish can't smell them inside the bubble any more than you can smell a peanut butter sandwich inside a Zip-loc bag. That made me very happy.

We don't sleep inside a bubble, but we have our own miracle. Jesus sends an angel, each evening, to surround us. We can sleep without fear, just like the Rainbow Parrotfish does inside its miracle bubble.

When Christ was crucified, I died with Him. Yet, I'm not dead, but alive because Christ lives in me. And the life I now live, I live by faith in the Son of God, who loved me and gave Himself for me.

Galations 2:20

The Giant Clam

One afternoon while diving in the South Pacific Ocean, I spotted a Giant Clam wedged in a crevice. The clam's two-sided shell sat partly open. I could see that soft flesh lined both sides.

"You are small now," I whispered to the clam, "You will grow to be a five hundred pound giant."

I looked the clam over, trying to discover a pincher it might use to reach out and snag a passing fish, or for a way it could suck in a lot of food from the water. That's when I noticed green flecks in the clam's body.

That's algae, I thought. Algae are green plants that need a place to live. It's a miracle that they can make food from bits of light that filter down into the sea. All this food makes the clam grow stronger and stronger. This is one of God's great ideas, I thought.

Another one of God's great ideas is that we can open our hearts and invite Him in. It's a miracle that He will live within us and make love and joy grow stronger and stronger in us.

www.ingramcontent.com/pod-product-compliance
Lightning Source LLC
Chambersburg PA
CBHW060843270326
41933CB00002B/179